Bed Time S
For
3 Years Old

This book belongs to:

Contents

Contents

The Adventures of Zog and the Bright Star

Once upon a time, in the near future, there was a distant planet in the galaxy called Glitteria. On Glitteria, among the shining stars, lived a little alien called Zog. Zog was different from the other aliens because he liked to wear a hat and had lovely freckles on his cheeks.

Zog loved looking at the stars in the night sky. Every night, he would climb a hill and look up at the firmament, dreaming of exploring distant galaxies.

One day, while Zog was exploring an alien forest, he saw something shining brightly among the trees. It was a shooting star! But, in reality, it was not a star, but a small spaceship. Inside the spaceship was a special visitor: Stella, a small Earth child.

Stella was a curious and courageous child who had landed on Glitteria by chance during a space trip with her family. Zog and Stella became friends immediately.

"Wow, you really are a funny little alien!" exclaimed Stella, looking admiringly at Zog.

"You're nice too, Stella!" replied Zog with a bright smile. "Would you like to explore my planet with me?"

Stella enthusiastically accepted and so their adventures began.

Zog and Stella explored luminescent forests, glided down crystal rivers and met extraordinary space creatures. Every day was a new discovery.

But then, one night, Zog and Stella saw a special star in the sky. It was different from all the other stars. It was bigger and brighter, and seemed to be sad.

"What star is that?" asked Stella.

Zog thought for a moment and then replied: 'It is the Bright Star, the brightest of them all. But she looks sad ever since I was born. I want to do something to make her smile."

Zog and Stella decided to help the Bright Star. They devised a plan to bring her joy. They collected pieces of fallen stars, shiny and colourful, and used them to create a huge glowing sign in the night sky. It said: "Bright Star, you are special!"

The news spread quickly among the inhabitants of Glitteria, and everyone gathered to see the surprise. When the Bright Star saw the message, she shone even brighter. She was happy!

"Thank you, Zog and Stella!" said the Bright Star gratefully. "You are truly special friends."

Zog and Stella smiled happily, knowing they had done something good. From that day on, the Bright Star shone with joy and every night the sky of Glitteria was even more enchanting.

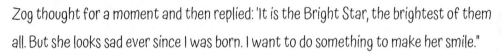

As time passed, Stella had to return to Earth. It was a sad moment for Zog, but they exchanged promises of eternal friendship and to meet again one day.

And so, Zog and Stella, having experienced extraordinary adventures together, proved that friendship and the desire to do good can light up even the saddest star.

d as Zog looked up at the night sky of Glitteria, he knew that even when you were far

ay, you could find a special friend in the stars.

d so it was that Zog and Stella learned that friendship and kindness can make the

rld, or even the galaxy, a better place for everyone.

Princess Luna and the Key of Dreams

Once upon a time, in an enchanted kingdom, there was a princess named Luna. Luna was different from the other princesses: she was not interested in glittering dresses or lavis parties. What she craved most of all in the world were stories.

Princess Luna loved to listen to the fairy tales told by her grandmother every night before bedtime. It was thanks to those stories that Luna had learnt the value of courag kindness and perseverance.

One day, while Luna was walking in the castle gardens, she found a secret door hidden among the roses. The door was small and silver, with a crystal key hanging beside it. Luna knew that this door led to a special place, but no one in the kingdom knew the key to open it.

Determined to discover what was hidden behind th mysterious door, Luna decided to embark on a journ She filled a small saddlebag with food, drink and a bc of her grandmother's stories, then put the key arou her neck like an amu

Luna passed through the castle gate and ventured into the enchanted forest. She walke for days, following the sound of the stream and the song of the birds. Finally, she came a huge waterfall. But the greatest surprise was what he saw behind the waterfall: a fai village!

The goblins, fairies and gnomes who lived there were surprised to see a princess in their kingdom. But Luna was not like the other princesses, and she was welcomed with affection. In return for her smile and kindness, the little beings told her that the key around her neck could open the Door of Dreams.

The Door of Dreams was a magical portal that took people into the world of dreams, an enchanted place where every dream became reality. Luna decided to go through the door to see what lay beyond.

When she entered the dream world, Luna found herself in a wonderful place. The mountains were made of candy, the trees were as tall as skyscrapers and the night sky was full of twinkling stars.

But there was one problem: the dream world was in danger. A dark dragon had stolen the key that kept the dream world alive. With courage in her heart, Luna decided to take action. She followed the dark dragon's footprints to his lair, where she found him holding the key tightly in his jaws. I

The dragon was fearsome, but Luna knew she had to be brave. With a kind word and a smile, she managed to convince the dragon to return the key.

Once the key was back in place, the dream world recovered. Luna returned to her kingdom with a heart full of gratitude for the stories that had inspired her courage.

When she returned to the castle, Luna shared her adventure with the kingdom and her grandmother. Now she had a new story to add to her collection of enchanting tales.

And so, Princess Luna learned that courage and kindness can open mysterious doors and even save whole worlds. And although she loved stories, she now knew that she could write her own stories of adventure and courage.

The Dromedary Who Wanted to Grow Up Fast

nce upon a time, in the heart of a vast, golden desert, there was a small camel
amed Samir. Samir was different from the other camels in his herd. While the other
amels were content to walk slowly across the sand dunes, Samir had one great
esire in his heart: he wanted to grow up fast.

amir felt small and impatient. He looked at the long legs of the adult dromedaries
nd dreamed of being as tall as them. Every day, he tried to walk faster, but his legs
ere still too short and clumsy.

ne day, while Samir was walking alone in the dunes, he met a wise old dromedary
amed Zahir. Zahir had been through many adventures in the desert and knew a lot
out life.

hy do you look so anxious, young Samir?" asked Zahir, looking kindly at the little one.
amir sighed and replied, "I want to grow up fast, I want to be like the other
omedaries. I want to run fast and see the world."

Zahir smiled wisely and said: "Little Samir, life is a journey, and the desire to grow fast will make you miss the wonders along the way. Everything has its time."

Samir was not sure he understood, but h[e] decided to listen to the old camel. Days an[d] weeks passed, and Samir began to see th[e] desert with different eye[s]

He began to notice the small wonders he ha[d] ignored before: the twinkling stars tha[t] appeared at night and the oases hidden in th[e] dune[s]

One day, while Samir was walking slowly, he heard a small sound coming from the sand. He dug with his snout and discovered a small egg. It was an ostrich egg, abandoned from its nest. Samir picked it up gently and carried it with him.
As Samir grew slowly, he took care of the egg with love and dedication. He kept it warm in the desert sun and protected it from night predators. When the egg finally hatched, a baby ostrich was born.

The friendship between Samir and the little bird grew every day. The little ostrich was called Rafiq and had long, fast legs. He taught Samir to see the desert from a different perspective and to run with the wind.

e day, when Samir had grown up and learned many lessons from his friendship with

fiq, Zahir came to visit him.

mir," Zahir said, "you have grown not only in height, but also in wisdom. Now you

lerstand that growth happens in the heart and mind, not just in the body."

mir smiled and nodded. He had learned that everything had its time, and that the

periences and friendships he had made along the way were more valuable than the

test ride.

om that day on, Samir was a happy and grateful camel. He was in no hurry to grow

quickly, for he knew that every day was a treasure to be lived to the full.

d so, the little camel Samir learned that true growth lies not only in height, but in

e, friendship and appreciating every moment of life's journey.

Tania the Turtle: In Search of the Island of Zakynthos

Deep in the ocean was a magical world inhabited by sea creatures of all shapes and colours. In this world, there lived a wise and gentle turtle called Tania. Tania was different from other turtles. She had a desire to travel to the island of Zakynthos, where she wanted to lay her eggs.

The island of Zakynthos was a wonderful place, but the journey would not be easy. Tania knew she would face challenges and dangers along the way, but her heart was set.

One day, with her strong and resilient shell, Tania set off on her journey. The first challenges she faced were the sea currents. The waters were rough and turbulent, but Tania swam with strength and determination. Thanks to her patience, she managed to overcome the currents and continue her journey.

As she swam deeper, Tania came across a school of luminous fish. They were fascinating and beautiful, but also a little intimidated to see a turtle in their waters for the first time. Tania reassured them with her gentle smile and continued her journey.

The sea creatures she met along the way told her about incredible places and fascinating stories. Tania was fascinated by their stories and felt richer with each encounter.

14

Tania's journey took her through a forest of swaying seaweed, where she had to face stinging jellyfish. Thanks to her caution, she managed to avoid them and continue on without injury.

Then, one day, the sky darkened and the wind picked up. A storm raged, and the waves turned into mountains of water. Tania felt frightened, but she clung to her dream with strength. After days of storm and struggle, the sky finally cleared, and Tania emerged from the water realising that she had survived one of the greatest challenges of her journey.

Then finally, she saw land on the horizon. It was the island of Zante! Her paws were tired but she could not have been happier.

Tania reached the beach and with great care began to lay her eggs in the warm sand. It was a special moment, two small tears of joy fell from her eyes and mingled with the waves of the sea.

As Tania watched her eggs, a group of Greek children saw her on the beach. They approached with sparkling eyes and radiant smiles. They were fascinated by the turtle.

Tania approached them politely and told them about her adventure. They all soon became great friends!

Tania stayed on the island of Zakynthos for a while, sharing stories and wisdom with the village children. Eventually, when her little turtles were born and grew strong, Tania knew that her journey to the beautiful island had come to an end.

With a heart full of love and gratitude, Tania said goodbye to the island and swam out to sea, ready for new adventures and new stories to share with her babies.

And so, Tania the turtle learned from this amazing journey that determination, kindness and courage can lead to the realisation of one's dreams, and that along the way one can make special encounters that make life even more beautiful.

The Adventures of Red and the Magic Book

nce upon a time, there was a little boy named Jacopo, who was nicknamed 'Red' by
eryone because of his bright red hair. Red was different from the other children in
s village. While the others played football or hide and seek, he loved to spend his
ıys between the pages of a book. He had a deep love for stories.

s library was his favourite place! It was a magical place, full of adventures,
ysteries and enchanted worlds. He spent hours reading books of all genres, but his
ıvourites were adventure and fantasy books. He dreamed of travelling through
ıntastic worlds and becoming a hero like those in his favourite stories.

One day, while leafing through an old book in his library,
he noticed a mysterious light coming from an old shelf.
Among old manuscripts and dust, he found a book unlike
any other. The cover was purple and shiny, and the title
was written in gold letters: 'The Magic Book of
Adventures'.

trigued, Red opened the book and began to read. With each page, the words came to
e, transporting him to a magical world. He found himself in an enchanted forest
ith elves and fairies, then in a kingdom of dragons and brave knights.

ıd was in ecstasy. He had finally found a book that allowed him to experience the
Iventures he had always dreamed of. He spent whole days immersed in the pages of
e book, travelling through fantastic worlds and making friends with extraordinary
ıaracters.

ıt one day, while in a world of pirates and hidden treasures, he discovered that the
ok had a problem. The pages began to fade, and the story was disappearing before
s eyes. The Magic Book of Adventures was in danger!

Red decided to do everything possible to save his book. He sought advice from a wise sorcerer, who told him that the only way to save the book was to find the Heart of Stories, a magical stone hidden in the realm of Lost Fables.

Without hesitation, Red set out on his journey to the realm of Lost Fables. He crossed stormy seas, explored dark forests and challenged terrifying monsters. Each challenge he encountered along the way made him more courageous and determined.

Finally, after many adventures, Red reached the realm of the Lost Fables. There, he found the Heart of Stories, a glowing, sparkling stone. The stone had the power to bring the pages of his book back to life.

With the Heart of Stories in his hand, Red returned to his world and used it to save the Magic Book of Adventures. The pages shone back to life, and Red was able to continue his adventures.

From that day on, Red knew that every page of a book was a door to a magical world. He had learned that even if he could not travel through fantastic worlds like his heroes, he could still experience incredible adventures between the pages of a book.

And so, Red shared his favourite stories with the other children in his village, inspiring each of them to explore enchanted worlds through the pages of books.

18

The Adventure in the World of the Future

nce upon a time, in a delightful town in central Italy, there were two curious and
dventurous children: Luca and Sofia. They had always been best friends and loved
ending their time exploring the world around them.

ne day, while exploring an old abandoned workshop, Luca and Sofia found a shiny
ver door. It seemed to have been forgotten by everyone. Intrigued, they decided to
en it and see what was on the other side.

en they walked through the door, they were speechless. They found themselves in
orld completely different from anything they had ever seen. The streets were
de of light and vehicles flew through the sky. It was a world full of advanced
hnology and incredible wonders. Luke and Sofia met a friendly robot named Robo
d, who guided them through the world of the future. They discovered that in this
rld, people had embraced technology to improve everyone's lives. There was no
re pollution, diseases had been defeated, and people were taking care of the
ironment.

But not everything was perfect. Robo Tod told them of a problem: a great distance separated the people of this world. They no longer communicated with each other as they once did, and friendships had become rare. Advanced technology had created a kind of social isolation.

Luca and Sofia realised that they had to do something to help the world of the future rediscover the value of human connections. They decided to organise a big friendship festival to bring people together and celebrate human relationships.

With the help of Robo Tod and the new friends they had met, they began to plan the festival. They built floating stages, organised light shows and played music that filled the air. The festival was a great success, and people began to smile, dance and make new friends.

But there was still a problem to be solved: many people were afraid of sharing their emotions and feelings. They were afraid of being judged by others. Luca and Sofia knew that they had to show people how important it was to be open and honest.

So, during the festival, they took the main stage and shared their feelings and stories with the audience. They told of their adventures and emotions, and encouraged everyone to do the same. In the end, many people felt inspired to share their stories, and the connection between people grew even more.

20

After the festival, Luke and Sofia decided to return to their world, but with hearts full of gratitude for the wonders they had seen and the friendships they had made. They had learnt that, even in a technologically advanced future, humanity and human connections were the most precious things.

They returned through the silver door, knowing that they would carry with them the message of the importance of human relationships in the world of the future.
And so, Luke and Sofia shared their incredible adventure with their world, inspiring everyone to connect, share and love, because friendship and love were the true treasure of the future.

The Tiger with a Different Coat

Once upon a time, in the deep jungle, there was a tiger named Flora. Flora was different from the other tigers of her kind. While the other tigers had a tiger-like coat with black and orange stripes, Flora had an entirely orange coat. This difference made her feel different and, often, very unhappy.

She looked at the other tigers with their beautiful tiger coats and longed to look like them. She was sad because she felt out of place among her peers. The other tigers often laughed at her, which increased her insecurity.

One day, as Flora was complaining to a wise old tortoise about her diversity, the tortoise said to her: 'Oh, little Flora, beauty is not only measured by external appearance. True beauty lies in the heart and soul. Your diversity is a special gift that only you possess."

Flora was not convinced, but decided to listen to the turtle's advice. She decided to go on a journey through the jungle to discover the meaning of diversity and learn to accept herself for who she was.

During her journey, Flora made new friends among the jungle animals. She learned that each of them had something unique that made them special.

he elephant had giant ears, the giraffe a neck so long it almost reached the sky, and
ie toucan with its beak much larger than its little head. Yet each of them was loved
id appreciated for their unique characteristics.

ne day, Flora met a black panther that had a strange white spot on its black coat.

he panther said to her: "Look, I too am different
om other panthers, but it is this very spot that
akes me special and unique. Diversity is an asset,
)t a defect."
ora reflected on what she had learned on her
urney and realised that diversity was no reason to
el sad or unhappy. She returned to her jungle with
ight heart and an open mind.

; she walked through the trees, she realised that her diversity was what made her
ique. Her completely orange coat was like a radiant sun that lit up the jungle. There
as no need to have tiger stripes to be a real tiger.
ie other tigers noticed the change in Flora. They no longer laughed at her; on the
intrary, they admired her self-confidence. Flora had learnt to accept and
ipreciate herself for who she was, and this made her radiant with happiness.
ir infectious happiness also inspired the other tigers. They began to realise that
/ersity was a wonderful thing and that each of them had something unique to offer
e world.

And so, Flora became a kind of guide for the other tigers, teaching them that beauty was not defined by outward appearance, but by kindness, self-confidence and the way one treated others.

Over time, the jungle became a happier and more harmonious place, where each animal was free to be itself without fear of judgement. Flora had demonstrated that 'diversity is also beauty,' and had turned her diversity into a source of strength and inspiration for all.

The Little Spice Craftsman

faraway land, amidst the enchanting landscapes of the Orient, lived a child named ir. Amir was different from the other children in his village. He was fascinated by fragrant spices growing in the surrounding fields and dreamed of becoming a ce artisan.

e village of Amir was famous for its aromatic spices. nilies cultivated fragrant gardens of cinnamon, ginger, meg and saffron. Spices made the village a magical ce, but Amir was much more interested in them. He amed of creating unique and delicious blends

One day, while walking through the spice fields, Amir found a mysterious plant. It as a variety of spice unknown in his village. Amir picked it and carefully brought it home. He began to experiment with the spice, mixing it with others and adding a pinch of creativity.

His spice blends were incredible. He created a golden, fragrant powder that made people dream of exotic flavours. His village was fascinated by Amir's creations, and he soon became known as the village spice artisan.
But his fame did not only reach the village. One day, a travelling spice merchant heard about Amir's extraordinary creations and decided to visit him.

25

He was a kind and wise man, with a beard as long and black as his deep, good eyes. H told Amir that he had the potential to become one of the greatest spice artisans in the East.

Amir, although happy for the opportunity, was reluctant to leave his beloved village. But the merchant convinced him that the world was full of wonderful spices and th he could share his passion with many different people.

So, Amir climbed onto the merchant's camel and together they began a journey through the Orient. They crossed golden deserts, passed through green oases and m people from different cultures, each with their own special spices.

Amir learned about the different spices of the Orient and his creations became mo and more extraordinary.

One day, while they were travelling, the merchant fell seriously ill. Amir took care o him with affection and attention. The merchant recovered thanks to Amir's care a as a sign of gratitude, gave him a precious bowl of golden spices.

Spezia dell' Amicizia

With it he created a magical mixture that could capture the flavours and aromas of the entire Orient. His blend became known as 'The Spice of Friendship' because it combined the best of each culture.

Amir returned to his home village with new knowledge and a heart full of experiences. He shared his adventures and discoveries with his village.

The 'Spice of Friendship' became famous throughout the village and beyond. People from all corners of the Orient travelled to taste it and smell its enveloping fragrance. Amir had realised his dream of becoming a spice artisan and proved that diversity could be a source of beauty and inspiration. His heart was filled with gratitude for the journey and the people he had met along the way.

And so, Amir's village became a place where spices told stories of friendship, sharing and love, and people from different cultures came together to celebrate diversity.

The Fisherman and His Faithful Companion Tobias

Once upon a time, in a quiet fishing village by the sea, there was a gentle fisherman named Luca. Luca was a man with bright eyes and an even brighter heart. Every morning, at sunrise, he would head out to sea in the hope of catching the biggest and most wonderful fish.

Beside him every day was his trusty companion, Tobia, a dog with reddish fur and affectionate eyes. Tobia always had a wagging tail and seemed to be Luca's best friend. Together, they were a formidable team.

Luke and Tobia shared incredible adventures as they cast their nets into the sea. They caught fish of all colours and sizes, but their dream was to catch a legendary fish that was said to be the biggest and most splendid of all.

One day, while they were out at sea, Luke felt the line pull hard. He strained and wrestled with the fish for hours. It was an epic battle between man and fish, but in the end, Luca managed to reel in the biggest fish he had ever seen. It was a brightly coloured fish with glittering scales.

ke was excited, but his heart was filled with compassion for the fish. He saw the
auty of this creature and did not have the heart to catch it. He decided to let it
turn to the sea, because he realised that the fish had to be free.

bia barked happily, as if he approved of Luca's choice. He was an extraordinary dog,
le to understand his master's heart.

om that day on, Luke and Tobia stopped looking for the legendary fish. Instead,
ey devoted their time to cleaning the beach of plastic and caring for the sea that
d given them so much. They realised that the true beauty of the sea was not just in
e wonderful fish, but in its purity and the love they had for it.

One winter, a violent storm hit the coast. The waves
were high and the wind howled. Luke and Tobias knew
they had to help. They dived into the rough waters
and rescued several sea animals trapped in damaged
fishing nets.

That night, the village gathered to thank Luke
and Tobias for their courage. They were
considered heroes for having saved so many
lives. But Luca and Tobia were simply happy to
have been able to help.

e years passed, and Luke grew old. By now, he was too old to go to sea. But Tobias
ver left him alone. He would sit beside him on the beach and look at the horizon
th his bright eyes. They were friends for life, sharing the joys and adventures of
e sea.

e day, while Luca was resting on the beach, he closed his eyes for the last time.
bia lay down beside him and looked at him with sadness. They had lived an
traordinary life together.

And at that moment, a group of fishermen from the village decided to honour the memory of Luke. They went into the sea and cast a net, but not to catch fish. They threw a net to clean the sea, just as Luke had done in life.

Tobias looked on with joy and approval. He had learned from Luke that there was beauty in loving the sea and helping others. He let a tear slide down his furry cheek, a a sign of gratitude for all they had shared.

And so, the story of the fisherman and his faithful dog, Tobia, became a legend in the village. They told the children the story of Luke and Tobias and taught them the val of loving the sea and the courage to do the right thing.

The Mystery of the Disappearance of the Village Chief

he heart of an enchanted forest, among the roots of tall
es, was a gnome village called Gnomelandia. In this happy
age lived the village chief, a wise gnome called Grandfather
rbagrigia. Grandpa Barbagrigia was respected by all the
abitants of Gnomelandia for his wisdom and kindness. But one
, something strange and mysterious happened.

e morning, as the sun's rays danced through the leaves, Gnomelandia awoke to find
t Grandfather Barbagrigia had disappeared! There was no trace of the village
ef, and the village was shrouded in an eerie silence.

tle gnome Carlo, a brave and curious boy, decided to solve the mystery together
h his trusted friends, Gigetto and Tiziano. Carlo was known for his cunning and
omitable spirit, while Gigetto and Tiziano were Carlo's best friends, always ready
help.

e three friends began to investigate the village, looking for clues that might lead
m to the solution of the mystery. Carlo, with his blue pointed hat and detective's
e, led the group with determination.

After hours of research and reflection, Carlo, Gigetto and Tiziano discovered an old spell book in the village library. With their ingenuity and cooperation, they managed to decipher the spell that would reveal the whereabouts of Grandpa Barbagrigia.

They followed the magic map that appeared from the pages of the book, crossing dark forests and the banks of mysterious rivers. Eventually, they came to a hidden cave, where they found Grandfather Barbagrigia, trapped by a dark spell cast by an evil sorcerer.

With courage and determination, Carlo, Gigetto and Tiziano defeated the sorcerer and broke the spell that held Grandpa Barbagrigia prisoner. Grandfather Barbagrigia embraced them with gratitude and pride, recognising the courage and wisdom of the young gnomes.

Back in Gnomelandia, the village resounded with joy and happiness at the return of their beloved village chief. Charles, Gigetto and Titian were celebrated as heroes and became the best friends of all the gnomes in the village.

And from that day on, Carlo, Gigetto and Tiziano continued to have exciting adventures in the village of Gnomelandia. Every day was a new mystery to solve, but with their spirit of friendship and cooperation, they knew that no challenge was too great for them.

And so, Gnomelandia continued to thrive thanks to the strength of friendship and the wisdom of Grandfather Barbagrigia, teaching all the gnomes that together, with love and courage, they could overcome any obstacle.

The Enchanted Journey of Bobo and Momi

Once upon a time there was a travelling painter named Bobo, who travelled the world with his faithful kitten Momi. Bobo was a talented artist, but what made him truly special was his ability to see the soul of the places he visited. With his magic brushes and vibrant colours, Bobo could paint not only landscapes but also the emotions and dreams of the people he met.

Accompanied by his kitten Momi, a cuddly kitten with curious eyes and a fluffy tail, Bobo travelled from village to village, bringing with him the magic of his paintings. Together, they explored faraway lands, imposing mountains and golden beaches, meeting people from different cultures and making extraordinary friends along the way.

Once, in the village of Rainbow, Bobo and Momi met an old gentleman called Grandpa Giulio. Grandpa Giulio was an old fisherman with wrinkled but bright eyes, who had spent his life contemplating the sea. Bobo decided to paint a picture of the sea for him.

While painting, Jacopo listened to Grandpa Giulio's stories of ocean adventures, turning those stories into vivid colours on the canvas.

In another village called Soleggiato, Bobo and Momi met a little girl called Lila. Lila had a radiant smile and eyes full of wonder at the world. Bobo decided to paint a portrait of Lila, capturing her joy and innocence in his painting. After seeing the portrait, Lila felt inspired to become an artist like Bobo and began to paint her adventures in the village.

n the golden desert of Golden Sand, Bobo and Momi met an ld merchant called Zahir. Zahir was a wise man who had ravelled for many years and collected treasures from every orner of the world. Bobo decided to paint a portrait of ahir, depicting him with his precious treasures around him. he portrait captured the wisdom in Zahir's eyes and his ve of knowledge.

t Bobo and Momi's journey was not only made up of picturesque landscapes and scinating people. One day, while they were in a mysterious enchanted forest, Bobo d Momi found an enchanted painting. The painting showed their home village, but ere seemed to be something wrong with it. The sky was grey, and the people ked sad.

ey decided to solve the riddle and, with the help of Bobo's artistic skills and Momi's riosity, discovered that the enchanted painting represented the future of their age if they did not continue to bring colour and happiness through their paintings.

Bobo and Momi returned to their village with a new determination. Bobo painted the walls of the houses in bright and cheerful colours, while Momi wandered around the village bringing joy and smiles to everyone. Soon, the village once again glowed with happiness and vitality.

But an unexpected ending awaited them. One night, as Bobo was painting the starry sky above the village, the stars began to shine brighter. Suddenly, a shooting star crossed the sky and touched his brush. Bobo felt a strange energy pass through him.

The next day, Bobo woke up to find that his paintings had come to life! Painted people danced in their paintings, animals ran free and landscapes moved with the wind. Bobo and Momi were happy and surprised. Their love of art had brought life into their world.

And so, Bobo and Momi lived happily ever after, continuing to travel, paint and bring life and joy wherever they went. Their story became legend in the world of artists, teaching everyone that art could bring magic and life to every corner of the world.

Isis and Adventure in the Heart of Ancient Egypt

ncient Egypt, between the lofty pyramids and the majestic River Nile, lived a
e princess named Isis. Isis lived in a lavish palace with walls of gold and attentive
vants, but despite all the luxury, her heart yearned for adventure.

One day, as she watched the sun set behind the pyramids
from the top of her tower, Isis decided it was time to
explore the world outside the golden palace. She had
heard of mysterious lands and fascinating people, and her
curiosity could no longer be suppressed.

the middle of the night, when the moon illuminated the desert and the palace
pt, Isis slipped out of her silken bed and opened the great secret doors of the
ace. With her heart pounding, she ventured out into the world outside.

s walked through the sandy desert, guided by the light of the stars and the wisdom
the wind. Along the way, she met a young spice merchant travelling with his cart
len with fragrant treasures. The merchant had eyes that shone like the stars and
entle smile.

e merchant told Isis stories of distant lands and people who lived in harmony with
ure. Isis was fascinated by his words and decided to join him on his journey.

Together, they travelled through cosy villages and vast deserts, meeting kind-hearted people and learning the ancient traditions of Egypt.

One night, during their journey, Isis and the merchant came upon an ancient temple hidden in the sand dunes. The temple was lit by scented candles and adorned with paintings of gods and goddesses. Isis felt drawn to the spirit of the place and knelt in prayer.

It was at that moment that Isis discovered the true meaning of her adventure. It was not just to see new places, but to discover the beauty of her people's traditions and spirituality. She had found a treasure even more precious than the gold of the palace the treasure of wisdom and connection with her people and the earth.

With a heart full of gratitude, Isis decided to return to the golden palace. She had learned that true wealth lay in the hearts of the people and in the traditions they kept alive. She returned to her kingdom bringing with her the gift of wisdom and love for her land.

When Isis returned to the palace, she did so with a radiant smile and sparkling eyes. She told her parents and all the people about her journey and the wonders she had discovered. The people were inspired by her words and began to value their traditions and their connection to the land even more.

And so, Isis became a wise and beloved princess, able to see the beauty of the world inside and outside the golden walls of her palace. As time passed, her kingdom prospered not only because of its gold, but because of the wealth of its people and the wisdom they had learned from the little princess who had dared to explore the heart of her world.

The Tailor and the King's Enchanted Robe

n the magical city of Venice, where canals whisper secrets and gondolas dance on
he water, there was a young apprentice tailor named Luca. He was a boy with
urious eyes and skilled hands, and worked in the workshop of the famous tailor
Master Antonio. Venice was abuzz in preparation for the carnival, the most
xtraordinary event of the year, and this year there was a special guest: King Ubaldo
the ruler of the eastern lands.

One morning, as the sun rose over the Grand Canal, Maestro Antonio turned to Luca
with a gentle smile. "Luca," he said, "you have shown great talent. I want you to create
special dress for our royal guest, King Ubaldo. It must be a masterpiece, something
hat will not only enchant the king, but also the entire city."

uca was trembling with fear, but his heart was swollen with excitement. He
mmediately set to work, looking for inspiration among the colours and fabrics of the
Venetian market. He traversed the narrow streets and secret corners of the city,
earching for the most precious and unique fabric he could find.

inally, among an intricate maze of colourful fabrics, Luca discovered a magical
abric. It was woven with golden threads and reflected the sunlight like a rainbow.
uca knew that he had found the special element that would make King Ubaldo's
ress unique.

With care and passion, Luca dedicated himself to his work. He spent days and nights sewing and embroidering, putting all his heart and soul into the garment. His work was imbued with love for his city and respect for the king who would come to visit.

The day of the carnival finally arrived. The city was in celebration, with colourful masks filling the streets and the cheerful melody of the musicians. King Ubaldo I arrived on his magnificent royal boat, greeted by a festive crowd. Luca, his hands trembling but full of hope, presented the enchanted dress to the king.

When King Ubaldo put on the robe, a magical hush fell over the crowd. The robe seemed to glow with a light of its own, as if the stars of heaven had fallen upon it. The king's eyes lit up with wonder and gratitude. "This is the masterpiece of a true artist," said the king in a moved voice. "Thank you, young tailor, for creating something so extraordinary for me."

The king's words were like a sweet melody to Luca's ears. His professionalism had been put to the test, and he had risen to the challenge.
Venice applauded the young tailor enthusiastically, recognising his talent and dedication.

But the dress had an unexpected magica power. When King Ubaldo walked the street of Venice, the dress radiated light and jo bringing smiles to the faces of everyone wh crossed his path. The magic of the dres spread through the city, bringing love an happiness to every corne hus, the carnival in Venice became even more magical thanks to Luca's enchanted 'ess. The young tailor had not only created a masterpiece of fabric, but had also 'ought love and happiness to his city. From that day on, Venice was known as the ty of the enchanted dress, and Luca became a respected hero, not only for his skill, t also for his kind heart.

nd so, the story of Luca and King Ubaldo's enchanted suit was passed down from neration to generation, teaching everyone that love and dedication in one's work n bring not only success, but also happiness to others.

Moon and Friendship in the Savannah

In the vastness of the remote South African savannah, under blue skies and bright sunshine, lived a small giraffe called Luna. Luna was tender and graceful, but also incredibly shy. Despite the abundance of playful cubs on the savannah, Luna could never make friends. She was always hiding in the tall grass, watching the other animals with shy, sad eyes.

One day, while hiding behind a bush, Luna heard merry laughter coming from a small group of cubs. There was Tembo, the curious hippo with a round belly, Zara, the lively tiger with bold stripes, and Raf, the brave rhinoceros with a majestic horn. Despite their differences, they were inseparable friends.

A small whisper of hope arose in Luna's heart. Perhaps, she thought, if she approache them, she could learn to overcome her shyness. With a heart full of courage, Luna decided to approach the group.

Tembo, Zara and Raf saw the little giraffe approach wi kind eyes and warm smiles. They paid no attention to h shyness; on the contrary, they welcomed her with joy. Teml told funny stories, Zara played hide and seek with her and R took her to explore the secret places on the savanna

Every day, the four friends met in the same place. Althoug initially shy, Luna began to feel more and more at ease wi the

42

had finally found friends who accepted her for who she was. Laughter became
most common sound in their secret clearing, and Luna learned to run, jump and
y without fear.

er time, Luna's friendship with Tembo, Zara and Raf grew even stronger. Together,
:y overcame challenges and adventures on the savannah, learning that
'severance and mutual help could overcome any fear. Luna was no longer the timid
affe she had once been; now she was brave, confident and full of love for her
ends.

e night, as they watched the stars in the twinkling sky, Luna smiled at her friends.
hanks to you," she said with gratitude in her eyes, "I have learned that friendship
n enlighten even the most timid heart. You are my family, and I will never forget
w kind you have been to me."

mbo, Zara and Raf smiled at Luna. "You are part of our family now," Raf said, "and
gether, there is nothing we cannot do."

d so, in the remote savannah of South Africa, four inseparable friends lived happily
d courageously. Luna had learned that with the help and love of friends, she could
ercome her shyness and discover the beauty of friendship. Now, whenever she saw
hy little giraffe on the savannah, she would extend a friendly paw, reminding her
at she would never be alone.

Sara's Submarine Journey

Once upon a time there was a sweet little girl named Sara, whose eyes shone like stars when she heard stories of the sea. Sara loved the idea of giant whales singing love songs, wise old turtles travelling through distant seas and corals as colourful as rainbows. The sea was her dream, and she longed to be a little mermaid for a day so she could explore those wonderful underwater secrets.

One night, while the sky was lit by thousands of star, small, bright sea fairy named Luminella descended fr the sky and gently landed on Sara's window. She was the to listen to children's wishes and turn them into real and Sara had such a pure and sincere wish that Lumine decided to help h

"Sara," Luminella said in a voice as sweet as the breeze, "I have heard your desire to explore the sea. I c help you. You will be a little mermaid for a da

Thanks to Luminella's magic, Sara woke up the next morning with a mermaid's tail and eyes shining with excitement. With a sinuous move, she dived into the ocean, immersing herself in the underwater world she had longed to see.

Under the water, Sara encountered extraordinary creatures. She swam with playfu dolphins that laughed like children, danced with jellyfish that shone like neon lights and hid in the crevices of colourful corals when a school of curious fish passed by. Every corner of the sea revealed a new wonder to her.

44

During her underwater journey, Sara also met an old sea turtle named Granny Wave. Granny Wave had seen many things on her long journey across the oceans, and with a gentle smile, she told Sara stories of the adventures and wisdom of the sea.

"The beauty of the sea is infinite, dear little mermaid," Granny Wave said in a warm voice. "But remember, the real magic is in the love we carry in our hearts for this world. Protect it and respect it always."
Sara nodded sagely, absorbing Granny Wave's every word into her heart.

As the day drew to a close, Sara returned to the shore. Luminella's magic dissolved, but Sara's heart was filled with joy and gratitude for the incredible experience she had had. Now, she had not only seen the sea world she so adored, but had also learnt the importance of love and respect for nature.
That night, Sara looked up at the starry sky and said a silent prayer of thanks to the magical fairy Luminella and all the sea creatures she had encountered. Her heart was filled with gratitude and love, and she knew she would carry those lessons with her forever.

And so, little Sara continued to love the sea and all its wonders, taking her love and respect for the underwater world with her every step she took on land. And every time she heard the call of the sea, she knew that, even if she could not always be a little mermaid, she would carry her underwater spirit with her, in the sweet melody of the waves and the vivid colours of the corals in her dreams.

Mark and the Secret of Balancing

In the quiet primary school 'Studia Bene', there was a lively boy called Marco. Marco loved to laugh, play and run around the playground, but there was one thing he really did not like to do: homework. For Marco, learning was like a grey cloud covering the sunshine of his fun.

One day, while Marco was looking for a place to hide t escape a maths assignment, he met Tommy, a diligen student with glasses and a love of books shining in h eyes. Tommy was not only good at school, but also kin and patient. He saw something special in Marco, eve though Marco himself did not know it ye

"Hey, why are you trying to hide?" asked Tommy, with a friendly smile. "Are you tryin to avoid homework?"

Marco nodded grimly. "I'd just like to play, Tommy. Homework seems so boring."

Tommy sat down next to Marco and smiled at him. 'I understand, Marco. I love playin too, but I've learnt that studying is like discovering new worlds! Do you want to try it together?"

So, they started studying together. Tommy made the homework more fun, with mathematical riddles and word games. Marco began to see the art hidden behind numbers and words, and suddenly, the grey cloud began to lift.

But Tommy not only taught Marco the importance of studying; he also taught him the importance of having fun.

fter completing his homework, Tommy would invite Marco to play football or run
ound the courtyard. He taught Marco that play and study could co-exist, creating a
rfect balance in his day.

ith time, Marco not only became good at school, but also a great friend. He learned
balance responsibility with fun, discovering that both were part of the adventure
lled life. His eyes now shone not only with play, but also with learning.

One day, during a science lesson, Marco raised his
hand enthusiastically and answered a difficult
question correctly. His teacher, Mrs Johnson,
smiled and said, "Congratulations, Marco! You
have really learnt a lot this year."

oking at Tommy gratefully, Marco smiled. 'Thank you, Mrs Johnson. And thanks to
mmy, I discovered that studying can be fun, but also that playing is important. It's
thanks to him."

mmy blushed slightly and smiled modestly. In that moment, they both knew that
ey had learned something special from each other: the importance of teaching and
rning, of leading and being led, and above all, the importance of balancing work and
y in everyday life.

d so, Marco became a bright and happy student, thanks to Tommy's friendship and
aching. Their story was an example of the power of kindness, friendship and
lance in every child's life.

Alfio's Adventures in the Bright Galaxy

In the far-off Bright Galaxy, where the stars danced like brilliant butterflies in the infinite sky, lived a little alien called Alfio. Alfio had curious eyes and a heart eager to discover the secrets of the vast galaxy. With him was his faithful little dog Pippi, a sweet and courageous companion on adventures.

Alfio had a mission: to explore the as yet unknown planets and share them with the rest of the galaxy. He had a special book, his 'Book of Wonders', in which he wrote down every planet he discovered. His dream was to make everyone aware of the beauty and diversity of the worlds he encountered.

One day, while navigating among the stars aboard his spaceship, Alfio saw a planet he had never seen before. It was shrouded in a golden light and seemed to emanate an extraordinary energy. Determined to find out what was hiding there, Alfio and Pippi ventured towards the mysterious planet.

As soon as they landed, Alfio and Pippi realised that the planet was inhabited by luminous creatures called Luminians. These beings were kind and welcoming, and showed Alfio and Pippi the wonderful secrets of their planet. There were trees that shone with their own light and flowers that changed colour with the mood of the wind. It was a magical place, and Alfio was enchanted.

48

ile exploring, Alfio and Pippi found an enchanted river. As they approached, the
er came to life, telling them stories of distant worlds and incredible adventures.
io decided that these stories should be shared with everyone, so he took out his
ok and began to write, noting down every word of the magic river.

io and Pippi's adventures took them to incredible places. They found a planet
ere trees grew upside down and another where the sky was always red like an
rnal sunset. Each new planet was an exciting discovery, and Alfio felt lucky to
e Pippi by his side, always ready to explore with him.

As they travelled from planet to planet, Alfio and Pippi
met other alien creatures eager to join their adventure.
Each time they added a new friend to their team, Alfio
noted their planet in his Book of Wonders. The book was
filling up with incredible stories, and Alfio knew he would
take these stories back to his galaxy for all to see.

en they eventually returned to their home in the Bright Galaxy, Alfio sat with his
ok of Wonders open in front of him. It was now filled with stories of distant worlds,
iting adventures and extraordinary friendships. With a smile, Alfio decided to
re his book with his entire planet. He wanted everyone to know that the universe
s full of wonders to be discovered, and that there were alien friends ready to
come them in every corner of the galaxy.

And so, the adventures of Alfio and Pippi became legends in the Bright
Galaxy. Every time they looked up at the night sky, the little dreamy
aliens could imagine the faraway worlds and fascinating stories that
lurked among the stars. And it all started with a little alien called Alfio
and his faithful four-legged friend, Pippi.

The Merry Adventures on the Happy Farm

On a cozy little farm called the Happy Farm, there is a magical world of friendly and fun animals. Every day, the farm animals have their own adventures while meeting new friends. Let's get to know these special characters together , shall we?

The day begins with the cheerful crowing of the Red Rooster, the lord of the farm. His cock-a-doodle echoes through the air, waking all the animals. Although it sounds like a normal sound, every morning the Red Rooster changes the tune, and all the animals wait for his crowing to find out what song he will sing that day.

After waking up, piglets Ric and Rac do their stunts the mud. They love to roll in the fresh mud because th say it makes their skin smooth and shiny. Every time y pass by them, they sprinkle some mud on you as a sign friendsh

Then there are the Lan and Lanette sheep, with their woolly, soft fleece. Every day they compete to see who can produce the most wool. Lanette is the fastest, but Lan is the most creative. They use their wool to create warm, fluffy blankets that keep other animals warm during cold nights.

In the chicken coop are the comical hens, Du Tuft and Roll. Duck is a big fan of myst novels and loves to read stories to the chic before bedti

uft loves to comb everyone's feathers, while Little Roll, as the name suggests, loves o roll on eggs to keep them warm. Each egg rolled by Roll became extraordinarily arge!

Let's not forget the cow Muccia, who provides fresh milk every day. But Muccia has a special talent: she can play the piano with her paws! Her sweet piano sounds fill the farm with melody, creating a magical atmosphere.

nd finally, there is the elderly cat Furfante, the wise nan of the farm. Furfante has traveled all over the world nd has lots of stories to tell. He is the friend most stened to by the other animals, and his adventures make he eyes of the little chicks and lambs sparkle.

)ays at the Happy Farm are full of surprises and laughter. The animals learn from ach other and share unique experiences. Every child who visited the farm feels)art of this big two-legged and four-legged family!

nd so, the Happy Farm continues to be a place of wonder and learning, where hildren can learn about animals and their extraordinary peculiarities. With fun tories and special friends, the farm is a magical place where each day brings new iscoveries and bright smiles.

The Mystery of the Missing Clock

In the hot summer of a small village, there lived a young inspector named Lara. She was a curious and bright child with sparkling eyes and raven hair. Lara was spending her holidays in her grandfather's old house, a mansion shrouded in an atmosphere of magic and secrets.

One day, while everyone was enjoying the summer sun, Lara discovered that her grandfather's beloved clock had disappeared. Grandpa Marco had kept it as a treasure, and now, the old clock that had given its sweet melody to the house had vanished into thin air.

Lara decided to investigate. Armed with a notebook, a magnifying glass and her cunning cat ZigZag, she began searching the house for clues. First she stopped Grandma Lucia, a kind lady with silvery hair and eyes that could tell many stories. The grandmother seemed genuinely surprised and saddened by the disappearance of the clock.

Little brother Giorgio was next on Lara's interrogation lis
With eyes wide with wonder and an ice cream in his han
Giorgio swore he had not touched the watch, although h
admitted he wanted to examine it closel

nen there was Giuliana, the domestic helper who had
orked for the family for years. Giuliana was a woman with
warm smile and gentle hands. Lara asked her if she had
oticed anything unusual, but Giuliana shook her head and
id she had seen nothing strange.

Finally, Lara faced the ZigZag Cat. With his almond-shaped
eyes and wavy tail, he always seemed to know everything.
ZigZag calmly wiped his muzzle, as if he was indifferent to
the mystery surrounding the clock.

it Lara did not give up. She continued searching, scanning every corner of the house.
; she examined her grandfather's study, a small drawer caught her attention. With a
utious movement, she opened it, and there, among old pens and notebooks, she saw
r grandfather clock, bright and beautifully restored.

Confused and surprised, Lara brought the watch into the
presence of her family. "But how did it get in here?" she
asked with wide eyes.

At this, Grandpa smiled tenderly. "I wanted to surprise you, dear
Lara," he said in a gentle voice. "I put the watch here because I
wanted to have it engraved for you. It was my birthday
present, a special gift for my curious and intelligent
granddaughter."

ra's eyes filled with tears of joy and emotion. The watch, now restored and
graved with a delicate floral pattern, shone in her hands like a precious treasure.
andfather had planned this as a surprise, a demonstration of his love and trust in
ra.

The family gathered around Lara, with loving smiles and sparkling eyes. Grandpa explained that he wanted Lara to know how special she was to him, how much he believed in her abilities and her enterprising spirit. The watch was a symbol of the precious time they spent together, but also of the time Lara would have to fulfil her dreams.

And so, Lara received her gift with gratitude in her heart. That watch would be more than just a timepiece; it would be an eternal reminder of her grandfather's love and trust in her.

The family gathered in a warm embrace, celebrating love, family and the wonder of the time they had together. The watch, now on Lara's wrist, continued to tick softly like a melody telling a story of love and family ties that lasted forever.

Ginetto's Sweet Success

ce upon a time, in a picturesque village, there was a confectioner named Ginetto.

etto loved to bake cakes, but every time he tried to create a new treat, he ended

making a mess in the pastry shop. With his hands kneaded with flour and a face full

sugar, he looked more like a snowman than a pastry chef!

spite his mistakes, Ginetto never gave up. He had a sweet heart and a burning

ire to learn. One day, while trying to bake a cake, the village's retired pastry cook,

saw him tinkering inside her pastry shop.

Lia had years of experience and a kind heart. Seeing Ginetto's determination, she decided to help him. "Come, dear Ginetto," Lia said with a loving smile, "I will show you the secrets to making delicious cakes."

iently, Lia taught Ginetto the secrets of pastry making: how to measure

redients with care, how to mix ingredients with love and how to decorate cakes

h creativity. Ginetto learned each step carefully, eager to improve.

s became weeks, and weeks became months. Ginetto kept practising, with Lia at

side. Every cake that burned or every biscuit that crumbled became a small step

ards success. Lia always encouraged him, telling him: 'The secret is practice and

sion, Ginetto. In time, you will become a great pastry chef."

One day, the village organised a big pastry competition. Ginetto decided to participate, buoyed by his growing confidence and Lia's valuable lessons. While working on his special cake, Ginetto thought about everything he had learnt.

When the day of the competition arrived, the village was filled with the delicious sm of freshly baked cakes. Ginetto presented his beautifully decorated cake, inspired b Lia's kindness and passion for baking.

When the judge tasted Ginetto's cake, his eyes lit up. "This is one of the best cakes I have ever eaten!" he exclaimed. The village erupted in applause, and Ginetto felt as he had just won a treasure.

From that day on, Ginetto became the most renowned confectioner in the village. Every morning, people queued up in front of his bakery, hoping to enjoy a slice of his delicious cake. Ginetto had learnt that no matter how many mistakes he had made the past, what really mattered was his dedication and willingness to learn.

And so, in the deliciously sweet-smelling village, Ginetto and Lia continued to make delicious delicacies together, proving that even the most bungling pastry chef could become a master in his art, thanks to the love, passion and invaluable help of a kind friend.

The Journey of the Flying Mickey Mouse

Once upon a time, there was a little mouse named Timo who dreamed of flying through the clouds like the birds in the sky. He gazed in admiration at the seagulls circling above his field, longing to join them on their journey across the wide world.

One day, as Timo scanned the sky with shining eyes, he saw a magnificent seagull called Paul landing right next to him. Timo, curious and fascinated by this majestic animal, approached and said: "Hi, I'm Timo! I would like to ask you a question, how do you fly so high?"

Paolo smiled kindly at Timo. "Hello, Timo! The key to flying is to believe in yourself and have a brave heart. Come with me, little friend. I will show you the world from a point of view you have never seen before."

And so, without hesitation, Timo climbed onto Paul's back and together they took off into the endless blue sky. The wind whistled in Timo's ears as they flew over snow-covered mountains, lush forests and shimmering oceans. Timo felt free as he had never experienced before.

On their journey, they met extraordinary creatures. There was Lila, a wise elephant with a kind heart who protected her family on the African savannah.

57

Then there was Kiko, a curious Australian koala who loved climbing trees. Each new friend taught Timo and Paolo something special about their world.

But the most exciting moment of the journey came when they arrived in a distant and mysterious land. There, they found an old owl named Horace who possessed a vast knowledge of the stars and the night sky. Horace taught Timo how to orient himself with the stars and how to find his way in the dark.

On starry nights, Timo and Paolo flew over continents and cities lit up like Christmas lights. They felt like family, united by the wonder of the world around them.

As time went by, Timo became more and more confident. With the help of Paul and their new friends, he learned that courage and self-confidence were the wings that allowed him to fly so high.

One day, when their journey came to an end, Paul said to Timo: "You have learnt to fly not only with your wings, but also with your heart, Timo. Now you are ready to face the world alone."

Timo looked at Paolo with gratitude in his twinkling little eyes. "I will be forever grateful to you for showing me the world and teaching me how to fly. I will never forget this adventure."

nd so, Timo got off Paul's back, but now he had something special inside him: the
owledge that he could fly not only physically, but also in his dreams and
pirations.

ith a bright smile, Timo greeted Paul and the friends he had met along the way,
owing that he had a life full of wonderful adventures ahead of him.

Regina's Magics and Special Friendship

Once upon a time, in the picturesque village of Salem, there was a lively little witch named Regina. Regina loved to do magic with her witch friends in the enchanted forest, where laughter and spells intertwined in the magical dance of colours.

One day, as Regina and her friends were playing in the trees, they saw a normal little girl named Lily who looked lost.

Regina, with her curious eyes and kind heart, approached Lily and said, "Hello, I'm Regina! Are you lost? Can I help you?"

Lily, her eyes wide with wonder, said shyly, "Yes, I got here by mistake. I don't know how I ended up in your village."

Regina smiled lovingly. "Don't worry, Lily! You are safe here. In our village, we welcom everyone with a kind heart."

Thus, Regina led Lily into the heart of Salem village, where the streets were paved with magical stones and the houses were adorned with bright star-shaped lanterns. Regina and her witch friends did their best to make Lily feel at home, showing her the wonderful spells they could do.

, although she did not have magical powers like the witches, was fascinated by
rything she saw. She watched spellbound as Regina made flowers dance in the air
1 created twinkling lights with a touch of her wand.

the days passed, Regina and Lily became inseparable. Regina taught Lily little
cks to feel part of the magical world, such as making shooting stars with a simple
ow wand. Lily, in turn, taught Regina to appreciate the beauty of simple things in
ordinary world, such as the warmth of the sun and the scent of flowers.

e day, as they were walking along the enchanted river, Lily asked Regina, "Can I
your friend, even though I am not a witch?"

jina smiled sweetly. "Of course, Lily! Friendship knows no boundaries. You are my
cial friend, even without magic."

m that day, Regina and Lily became inseparable.
jina showed Lily the secrets of magic, and Lily taught
jina the power of friendship and love. Together, the
ated a bond that shone like the stars in the night sl
village of Salem, once reserved only for witches,
ned up to new friendships and experiences. Regina
proved that friendship could overcome all differer
that the greatest magic of all was that of love and
eptance.

And so, in the magical village of Salem, Regina and Lily continued to have enchanting adventures, proving to the world that friendship could create spells more powerful than any magic in the world.

And in both of their hearts, their friendship shone like a bright star, lighting the way for all who sought love and acceptance.

The Adventures of the Old Notebook

Once upon a time, in a dusty attic of an old house, there was a lonely old notebook. It was a special notebook, but it was sad because no one had ever written anything about it. It lay there, forgotten, with no story to tell.

One day, a curious little girl named Sofia ventured into the attic. Her eyes sparkled with wonder as she explored the forgotten objects and memories buried beneath the dust. Among the objects, she discovered the old notebook.

"Oh, you are so beautiful," Sofia said, stroking the worn cover. "I wonder how many wonderful stories you could tell."

The old notebook trembled slightly, as if he had heard Sofia's kind words. It was the first time someone had spoken to him with affection. He decided it was time to begin his adventure.

With great excitement, Sofia opened the notebook. The sheets were blank, ready to receive the words and adventures that were to come. She sat by the window with a pencil in hand, ready to write the first story in the old notebook.

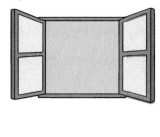

Sofia began to write fervently, creating fantastic worlds and magical characters. The old notebook absorbed every word, transforming it into vivid images and exciting adventures.

63

Sofia invented stories of flying dragons, brave princesses and hidden treasures. The old notebook danced with joy through Sofia's words.

As time passed, Sofia and the notebook became inseparable. Every day after school, Sofia ran to the attic to write down new stories. The notebook was happy to finally have a voice, and Sofia's stories gave it life.

Sofia's words created enchanted worlds, but they also had a magical power. The stories she wrote in the old notebook taught valuable lessons about kindness, friendship and inner strength. Sofia and the notebook became not only friends, but also companions on adventures.

One day, while Sofia was writing a story about the courage of a little mouse, the notebook flickered once again. This time, however, it was not out of sadness. It was from gratitude. It was gratitude to Sofia for giving it meaning, for filling it with stories and love.

With time, news of the magic notebook spread through the neighbourhood. Children came from all over to hear the incredible stories of Sofia and her special friend. The old notebook had finally found its place in the world, as the guardian of wonderful adventures and a source of inspiration for everyone.

nd so, the old notebook, once abandoned and lonely, became the centre of joy and eativity in the lives of many. Thanks to Sofia's love and imagination, the old tebook was no longer sad. It had become the guardian of dreams, the link between ntastic worlds and the kind heart of anyone who dared to open it.

Milù and Pepe: A Lesson on Hygiene

In sunny Sicily, on Nonna Rosa's farm, lived two special friends: Milù, the pretty white cat, and Pepe, the friendly and somewhat mischievous little dog. Milù always liked to be clean and tidy, while Pepe preferred to play in the countryside, happily rolling around in the mud. Pepe hated the idea of a bath and thought running around dirty was great fun.

One day, as the warm sun shone in the blue sky, Milu decided it was time to teach Pepe the importance of personal hygiene. Seeing Pepe all dirty with mud, Milù approached with a gentle smile.

"Pepe," Milù said in a calm voice, "it is important to stay clean. Bathing is not only to look nice, but also to stay healthy and happy."

Pepe frowned. "But Milu, mud is so much fun! I don't want to take a bath."

Milu smiled lovingly. "I understand that, Pepe, but having a clean coat and healthy skin is important for all animals. It helps prevent disease and makes us feel good."

Despite Milù's kind words, Pepe was not convinced. However, that evening, when the sun had lowered to the horizon, Milu had a brilliant idea. He took Pepe near the small waterfall in the farmyard.

"Look, Pepe," said Milu, showing him the cool water flowing from the waterfall. "The water is natural, refreshing and helps us stay clean. Here's a fun way to take a bath together!"

e looked at the water with curiosity. Slowly, he approached and touched the
ter with one paw. He was hesitant at first, but then, seeing Milú playing in the
terfall, he decided to follow her. With a playful laugh, Pepe began to play with Milú
he cool water.

t night, when Pepe lay down in his kennel, he felt strangely satisfied. He had had a
of fun taking a bath with Milu. From that day on, Pepe began to see bathing as
ething fun and no longer as a duty.
time went by, Pepe learned to enjoy his bath every evening. Milú showed him how
sonal hygiene could not only be necessary, but also fun. Whenever Milu and Pepe
ed in the waterfall, they laughed together and learned from each other.

so, on Grandma Rosa's quiet farm, Milú and Pepe became a living example of the
ortance of personal hygiene. Their friendship taught the children of the farm and
readers of this story that taking care of yourself can be a fun adventure,
ecially when you have a special friend by your side.

The Spectral Adventure of Marco, Pietro and Elisa

In a quiet town, lit by the full moon on Halloween, lived three little friends: Marco, Pietro and Elisa. This curious trio had heard scary stories about the old abandoned house at the end of the street. They said it was haunted, but Marco, Pietro and Elisa's curiosity was greater than their fear.

That Halloween evening, with their colourful costumes and bags of candy in hand, they decided to finally discover what was hidden behind the barred doors of the mysterious house. With uncertain steps and beating hearts, they ventured out into the darkness.

When they entered the house, they heard a strange hissing in the wind. The house looked like a labyrinth of dusty rooms and dark corridors. As they explored, they heard creaks and strange noises coming from the walls. But their courage did not desert them.

Suddenly, a faint light guided them to a hidden room. Inside was a dusty old book. Marco, the bravest of the group, decided to open it. Inside were spells, maps and tales of ancient spirits. They were so absorbed in their reading that they did not notice that the room was slowly lighting up with a soft, golden light.

Gradually, the book began to tell them the history of the house. They discovered that the house had once belonged to a kind witch named Isabella.

She had never been evil, just lonely. When the three friends realised that the house was not haunted, but simply neglected, they decided to help Isabella's ghost find peace.

With tenacity and initiative, Marco, Pietro and Elisa began to clean up the house. They swept away the dust and fixed the broken furniture. As they did so, the house began to shine again. The old objects seemed to smile with joy.

The moment they finished, a warm glow enveloped the room. The image of Isabella, the gentle witch, appeared. In a soft voice, she thanked her three friends for bringing light into her home and heart. As thanks, Isabella gave them a magic potion that would fulfil one of their wishes.

Marco, Pietro and Elisa looked into each other's eyes and realised that their wish had already been granted: they had found a special friend in Isabella and had discovered that even behind frightening appearances could hide something beautiful.

So, with hearts full of gratitude and happiness, the three friends left the abandoned house that Halloween night. The house was no longer spooky, but rather a place of warmth and love.

And from that night on, Marco, Pietro and Elisa told their adventure to the village children. Every Halloween, the story of the gentle witch Isabella and her brave friends was told, reminding everyone that behind every scary thing there is always a sweet surprise.

And so, the quiet little town lived on with the magic of friendship and the courage to look beyond appearances, just as Marco, Pietro and Elisa had done that magical Halloween night.

Dear parents and beloved children,

Today, as we have reached the end of this magical adventure of words and images, I would like to express my deepest gratitude. It has been an extraordinary journey, an enchanted journey through the pages of these fairy tales, and all of this was possible thanks to you.

To the parents who dedicated their precious time to reading these stories to their little treasures, I want to say thank you. Thank you for nourishing your children's imaginations, for accompanying them into fantasy worlds and for creating unforgettable moments together.

To the children, the true protagonists of these stories, I want to say thank you for allowing me to enter your dreams and fantasies. I hope you found comfort in the pages of these tales, that you smiled with the characters, and that you learned important life lessons as you journeyed with them.

Stories are like little magic lanterns that guide us through the darkness of life, and you have allowed these lights to shine even brighter. Every word written was inspired by the love I have for you, for your curiosity and your joy.

Thank you again, from all my heart, for allowing me to share these stories with you. May the magic of fairy tales continue to shine in your lives, illuminating every dark corner and bringing joy and serenity.

With eternal affection, Penelope Your Storyteller